A PLUM JOB

A PLUM JOB

How to Obtain a Political Appointment in Washington, D.C.

by
John W. Anderson

Chameleon Press
Kansas City, MO
chameleonsartskc.org

copyright 2018 John Anderson
1st Edition: 11 9 7 5 3 2 1
ISBN: 978-0-9990222-6-9
Library of Congress Control Number: 2018954214

design: Jeanette Powers
cover photo: US Fish & Wildlife, Public Domain (CCO)
bio photo: Bush Administration Photograph
plum image: Pierre-Joseph Redouté

Common plum (Prunus Domestica)

TABLE OF CONTENTS

*This guide is dedicated to my children Jay, Jill and Jeni.
This is just another chance to let you, and everyone
who reads this, know how much I love you.*

ACKNOWLEDGEMENTS

The idea for this guide originated in 1999 when I wrote the initial version while living in Washington, D.C. and was working within the George H.W. Bush administration. From my opportunity to serve as a political appointee and in the afterlife of my service, I realized that many others share the desire to experience government and politics from inside the beltway but have no idea how to go about it. So, for those that do have such an interest, I am providing this information to help guide them through the maze.

I want to thank my good friends Bud and Ginger Albright for continually encouraging me to share my experience. As the many drafts were written and edited, I want to thank friends, both inside and outside of politics, for their encouragement and time to offer valuable suggestions. This is as much your product as it is mine.

Thank you very much Rosamond Brown. My sincere appreciation also goes to fellow political junkies and authors Jeff Lord and Craig Orfield. Many thanks also go to Bill Bartalone, Jamir Couch, Dr. Bo Denysyk, Ken Ferguson, Dan Flynn, Ken George, George Kopp, Meg Losty, Geoff Merrill, Nancy Ramsden, John Renken, Lottie Shackelford, Richard Steinkamp, Earl Whipple, Juan and Kim Woodroffe, Deborah Yarbrough, Steve Snitz, Greg Patterson and Maggie McCoy (my special love).

A special thanks goes to Jeanette Powers in Kansas City. Jeanette was invaluable with her creative publishing skills, including the cover design and the layout of the book.

INTRODUCTION

Have you ever been curious about what goes on inside your government and how folks get those "plum" jobs? Have you ever thought about living such an experience yourself? Would you like to obtain a political appointment? If so, the time to get started is now.

You will ask yourself, am I qualified? What do I do? Who do I call? Who do I write? Who do I see? Who will help me? How long will it take? Do I have a chance? What's the salary? Is it for me?

We hear about our government each day on television, in the newspaper and online. We talk among our family and friends about current events. A few of the political players become household names. But for the most part, the business of government is conducted by a silent legion of public servants. Based on a report by the Washington Post, as of December 2016, there were about 9,000 such positions in Washington, D.C., of which approximately 4,000 were politically appointed.* These appointees are men and women chosen by the President or by the senior policy makers and management within the various agencies of the Federal Government. They form the spine of each administration.

The United States Government Policy and Supporting Positions (more commonly referred to as *The Plum Book*) is published by the Senate Committee on Homeland Security and Government Affairs and the House Committee on Government Reform alternately after each Presidential election. It lists the 9,000 Federal Civil Service leadership and

* These numbers and specific positions will vary from administration to administration.

support positions in the Legislative and Executive branches of the Federal Government.

The Plum Book was first published in 1952 during the Dwight Eisenhower administration. With a touch of humor, someone at the original publishers decided the book should have a purple or plum-colored cover to reflect that it contained the "plum" political appointee jobs, and the tradition has stuck ever since.

For the twenty prior years, the Democratic Party controlled the Federal Government. When Eisenhower took office, the Republican Party requested a list of the government positions that the new President could fill. The next edition to *The Plum Book* appeared in 1960 and has since been published every four years just after the Presidential election.

Political positions in the three branches of the Federal Government will possibly change hands at the end of a presidential term. This is especially true if there is a change in the presidency, and almost certain if the new president is from a different political party, regardless of party affiliation.

According to the Government Printing Office, there are three categories of federal political appointments:

1. PAS: Presidential Appointments with Senate confirmation. These positions include senior leaders, cabinet secretaries and their deputies, the heads of most independent agencies and ambassadors.

2. PA: Presidential Appointments without Senate confirmation. These positions include much of the White House

staff as well as various positions scattered throughout some of the smaller agencies.

3. SC: Schedule C Appointments. These positions serve in a confidential or policy role. (for more info: see p. 24)

This guide will give you detailed answers to your questions. It will walk you through the process in an easy to understand way. It will also help you determine whether or not the enlightening and rewarding privilege of a political appointment is right for you. See what you think.

MY STORY

Good fortune was with me as I grew up in Prairie Village, Kansas, a wonderful, middle-class suburb of Kansas City. I was the only child of my loving parents. School took me to the University of Kansas where I graduated from the School of Journalism before attending graduate Business School. One of the highlights of my college days was the opportunity to be a member of the Sigma Chi fraternity where several close friendships were developed. Many of these friendships exist still today.

My professional career began as a stockbroker with a local Kansas City firm that was later acquired by Paine Webber Jackson and Curtis. This opportunity was created through a Sigma Chi alumnus who had befriended and counseled me during my years at KU. Success provided me the opportunity to move to Tulsa, OK in order to open a new office for Paine Webber.

I had not been involved in politics, but as time passed, I became more and more involved in the Tulsa community. We met some wonderful people and made many new friends. As it turned out, some of these friends were involved in the political world. One was a state representative and was later elected to the U.S. House of Representatives. Another was the Tulsa mayor who eventually became a U.S. Senator. Both are still in office today. A close friend, Frank Keating, was a local attorney who later ran for and was elected governor of Oklahoma. Frank is now retired.

In January of 1989, George H.W. Bush took office

as the President of the United States. Shortly thereafter, Frank was offered the position of General Council for the Department of Housing and Urban Development (HUD). The primary mission of HUD is to develop cost effective ways of delivering housing assistance to those in need that not only helps them today but creates a pathway to self-sufficiency for them tomorrow. Past NFL quarterback, Jack Kemp, was the HUD Secretary. Jack was a quality public servant and a fantastic fellow. He would have also made us all proud as our president. Jack passed away just a few years ago and we all miss him dearly.

Frank accepted the offer and moved to Washington, D.C. About this same time, I was going through a divorce. Frank and I continued to stay in touch. Shortly after he accepted his new position at HUD, Frank asked me if I would like to come to Washington D.C. and join the team. With my political activities in Tulsa, coupled with my experience in securities and multi-family residential properties, I was a good fit. But, without Frank's support, this opportunity would not have presented itself. I moved to Washington, D.C. in 1990. Specifically, I lived in Old Town Alexandria, VA, which is a beautiful, historic town. Plus, it was only a short walk to the Metro that took me to work every day. It was wonderful.

My time at HUD was an irreplaceable experience. I was exposed to the business side of HUD, as well as the intricacies of how government operates. HUD provides a genuine service to America's lower income population. It was also a good representation of government bureaucracy. Secretary Kemp dealt with the policy and political side of our agency and we political appointees were charged with both the task of supporting the Secretary and of helping to implement HUD policies.

Sometime after I joined HUD, I was asked to accept the position of Deputy Administrator at the General Services Administration (GSA). The responsibility of GSA is to save the tax payer money by supplying prudent management of federal real estate assets and to provide efficient and effective acquisition solutions across the Federal Government. Being the Deputy Administrator, my primary responsibility was focused on supporting the Administrator with the implementation of his policies.

After President Bush left office, I left government service as the new administration arrived, but I remained in Washington, D.C. I became involved with various multi-family residential real estate projects and remained very active in politics.

In 2001, I decided to go back home to Kansas City. As much as I loved Washington, D.C., I felt that it was just time. I then joined Prudential Insurance in order to form a new company called Prudential Lofts and Condos (PLC). The purpose of PLC was to promote and sell condominiums in Kansas City's downtown area. A few years later I left PLC and created the John Anderson Company (JACO), whose mission was to work with Kansas City, Missouri's municipal government in promoting downtown development and with the city's urban multi-family developers in the financing of their projects through equity investors. At this time, few people lived in downtown Kansas City. Mayor Kay Barnes and I were two of the few who believed in the potential for downtown living in Kansas City. It took a while, but downtown today, in addition to being a bustling commercial center and having a new street car system, is thriving with many restaurants and entertainment venues. Thousands of residents are living downtown and enjoying urban life. Thank you, Mayor Barnes.

A couple years after I came back to Kansas City, I met Maggie McCoy. Soon after meeting Maggie, I joined her on the Kansas side of the state line in Johnson County and we have been together ever since. I retired in 2010, but have continued to stay active in local, county, state and national politics on both sides of the state line.

My government/political background has been invaluable. Plus, it has been fun. I made countless friends through my political involvement in Washington, D.C. It all started in Tulsa and has continued here in Kansas City. Many of my friends from the "Hill" are still in Washington, D.C. Several of us continue to keep in touch and remain in each other's lives. What a blessing. Strong friendships are an invaluable part of life.

Well, I have given you my personal experience as a political appointee. Hopefully you will be able to relate my story to your own desires and political goals. If you decide to pursue a Federal, State or Local political appointment, this guide will provide you with a road map on how to proceed. If it feels right, go for it.

The Experience and Categories of Government Service

Working for the Executive Branch of the Federal Government in Washington, D.C. can occur in one of two basic forms. You can be a career Civil Service employee hired through a competitive process and not affected by politics or change in administrations. This group represents by far the largest segment of government workers. And, as the name implies, the Civil Service employee tends to work for the government for the long term. For example, at HUD, it would be a Civil Service staff person who would be dealing with a developer of a government subsidized housing project. At GSA, a Civil Service employee would likely be responsible for negotiating a government lease in a commercial office building. The second type of government employee is the political appointee who is hired directly by the current administration based on his/her political loyalties and activities, along with his/her political work experience. The former represents the continuity and much of the core, institutional knowledge within a given agency and they deserve much credit for their devotion in helping make government work. The latter of the two represents the policy makers and management. The purpose of this guide is to look into the detailed process of entering this latter group: the political appointees.

Opportunities exist within the White House and among a wide range of government departments and agencies. Among others, these generally include the Departments of Agriculture, Commerce, Defense, Education, Energy, Health and Human Services, Housing and Urban Development, Interior, Justice, State, Transportation, Treasury and Veteran Affairs. Other positions are also included in the Executive Office of the President such as the Office of Management and Budget, the U.S. Trade Office, the National Security Agency, the Central Intelligence Agency, the Federal Bureau of Investigation, the National Security Council and the Council of Economic Advisers.

In addition, the government consists of close to 100 independent agencies such as the Environmental Protection Agency, Equal Opportunity Commission, Export-Import Bank of the U.S., Federal Communications Commission, Federal Deposit Insurance Corporation, Federal Election Commission, Federal Emergency Management Agency, Federal Maritime Commission, Federal Reserve Commission, General Accounting Office, General Services Administration, Government Printing Office, Library of Congress, National Aeronautics and Space Commission, National Archives and Records Administration, National Labor Relations Board, National Science Foundation, National Transportation Safety Board, Nuclear Regulatory Commission, Occupational Safety and Health Review Commission, Office of Government Ethics, Office of Personnel Management, Peace Corps, Postal Rate Commission, Railroad Retirement Board, Securities and Exchange Commission, Selective Service Commission, Small Business Administration, United States Information Agency and the United States Postal System.

Lastly, there are several Non-Governmental Organizations (NGOs) you might be familiar with, such as the American Red Cross, Federal National Mortgage Corporation, Inter-American Development Bank, International Monetary Fund, National Railroad Passenger Corporation (AMTRAK), Organization of American States, Securities Investor Protection Corporation, Smithsonian Institute, and the United Nations. The majority of NGOs, but not all, are designed to be apolitical and for the most part are not good candidates for political appointments.

Within the above agencies and organizations, there are many departments that you may find interesting and of particular relevance to your background. For example, The Office of the Secretary, i.e., Secretary of State, sounds exciting, but is it a place you want to work? You would be close to the action, but unless you are the chief of staff, speech writer, executive secretary or scheduler, you would basically be a bag-carrier, doing travel advance work. This of course can vary depending upon the management style of the Secretary. The Office of Congressional Affairs handles an agency's activities with members of congress and their staffs, which includes a lot of correspondence and casework. The Office of Inter-Governmental Relations is an agency's liaison with states and local governments. The Office of Public Affairs will coordinate all activities with the media, and the Office of Equal Opportunity works with minority issues. There is an Office of General Council that deals with legal issues.

Each agency will also have several departments that are related to its specific business. An up-to-date listing of these various entities and the specific jobs and relative pay grades are available and each can be found in *The Plum Book*. As mentioned earlier, every four years, just after the presidential election, *The Plum Book* is published alternately by the House Committee on Governmental Reform and Oversight and the Senate Committee on Government Affairs. You can find a copy online and in many local libraries.

As discussed in the Introduction, there are several categories of political appointments relative to levels of responsibility that are described in *The Plum Book*. There are three most common types: The Presidential Appointment with Senate Confirmation (PAS) is the most senior type of appointment; the Presidential Appointment without Senate Confirmation (PA); and the third and most typical type is the Schedule C Excepted Appointment (SC). SC's represent some mid-level and all entry-level appointments. Persons in Schedule C positions are typically appointed by PAS or PA appointees rather than by the President. However, SC posts must be reviewed and approved by the Executive Office of the President.

Schedule C individuals typically serve as confidential policy advisers and have volunteered for the transition team, for the Presidential campaign, know someone who is on their way to being an undersecretary or an assistant secretary, or are someone who is already working for an appointee and gets brought along. It is assumed that the SC appointee is sympathetic to the president or was brought to the job with thorough knowledge of the supervisor's goals and priorities. In addition to the political agenda, the Policy and Public Outreach (PPO) and the White House Liaison Office want to know that you believe in the Mission of the United States of America, the government, the president-elect and their incoming team.

Another government employee category is the Senior

Executive Service (SES). Most SES positions are filled by senior Civil Service employees whose jobs are not likely to become subject to political appointment.

25

Some of the larger federal agencies, thus employment possibilities, are the Defense Department, the State Department, the Justice Department, the Homeland Security Department, the Energy Department and the Treasury Department. Each of these agencies have specific titles and levels of responsibility. During my time at GSA, I was the Deputy Administrator. In order to illustrate the depth of politically appointed positions in a typical federal agency, I have listed below such appointment positions at GSA:

Administrator

Deputy Administrator

Chief of Staff

General Council

Commissioner-Federal Acquisition Services

Commissioner- Public Buildings

Associate Administrator-Communication

Associate Administrator-Policy

Associate Administrator-Small Business

Associate Administrator-Office of Government Affairs

Associate Administrator-Civil Rights

Associate Administrator-Mission Assurance

Chief Human Capital Officer

Chief Information Officer

Chief Financial Officer

Chief Customer Services

Ten Regional Administrators

This list contains 25 politically appointed positions at GSA. One can now see why *The Plum Book* contains approximately 4,000 such positions when all of the 305 government departments and agencies are considered.

Working as a political appointee within the Executive Branch of our government opens an entirely new world to the first-timer. There is a warm and fuzzy side that evokes a feeling of patriotism to your country and pride within yourself. The appointee finds him/herself immersed in events that are commonly seen in the daily news. To know that you are contributing to your country's operations by helping to shape and implement America's policies is a rewarding feeling. To be exposed to the leaders of your country, and possibly to those of foreign nations, is euphoric and exciting. The appointee has the opportunity to meet many fascinating people, some of whom will become lifelong friends. This has certainly been true in my case. Some of these friends are still in Washington, D.C. and others are scattered around the country. Photographs from the past, telephone calls, emails, birthday cards and personal visits to and from my D.C. friends are really special and irreplaceable. Friendships are the glue that binds us all.

Before you take the plunge into the government, keep in mind that there are cautions to consider as well. Be aware that you are entering a seemingly bottomless bureaucracy where decisions and progress can be laboriously slow. Frustration is common. You enter the new job with great enthusiasm born through both love of country and a belief in a particular political policy agenda. You believe that your entire agency will be one big supportive team all working toward a common goal. Unfortunately, this is sometimes not the case.

There will be two "teamwork" issues. First, while an appointee will likely receive a welcome smile from the career folks, he/she will undoubtedly find that they are not always in full agreement with the agency's current leadership and agenda. Remember that many of the career staff have probably been there a long time and have existed through numerous administrations, but profess disparate policies on the issues relative to past administrations. Thus, these people have learned to float along at an even keel and play a supportive role for the current appointees. Again, their work is invaluable to government.

You will find the "system" can proceed at a snail's pace and sometimes crumble under its own weight. Patience and diplomacy will become some of your most valuable attributes if they aren't already. The relationship between the career and political people is a curious but important one. In one respect this all seems backwards. Those with the power and policy-making authority are the new guys, the "short-termers", and the career employees with the tenure and experience play a more supportive role. If the appointee remembers where the historical knowledge base is and treats the career staff with the respect they deserve, he/she should get along fine.

The second issue will be found among your own team of appointees. You will soon find that different individuals and often times, even groups, will splinter off while promoting their own agenda over the good of the team. Now before you say, "how could they," remember that you are now in the world of politics. By their very nature, people can be territorial beings. It may not be that much different from the "real" or "outside" world but it will seem more pronounced because of the environment in Washington, D.C. Remember you are there because of politics. So, don't let this worry you. Just be aware of it. Deal with this issue but concentrate on doing a good job for your agency, your political party, your administration and the taxpayer.

Enjoy every minute of your experience. It's the chance of a lifetime.

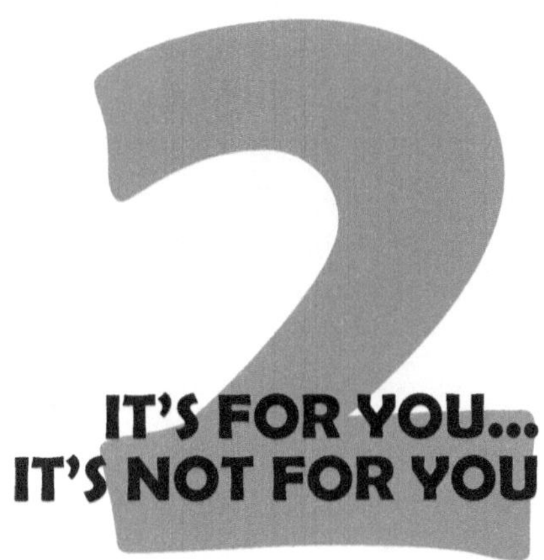

Many questions need to be answered before one accepts a political appointment. You will weigh your own qualifications. Yes, it would be a fabulous learning experience. You would learn how the political system works as well as the inner-workings of your particular agency. You would learn how Washington, D.C. works and how government operates. I use the term government in the sense that it includes all three branches, the political parties, the relationship with state governments and the lobbying community. The latter definitely extends out into the colonies (that's D.C. speak for the 50 states) and is an integral part of government workings. It is safe to say that lobbying effects many executive and legislative decisions.

You will feel, and possibly actually have, some degree of power. While this can be a good thing, it also connotes responsibility, hard work and caution. First of all, you would be being paid by the taxpayer and thus you are most obligated to do your best work on their behalf. In many cases you will be making more money than the career people. The career employees will go home at 4:30 PM. You will often be there until 6:30 PM or later. Some career employees may have accumulated tons of leave time and retirement benefits. Depending on their tenure, some will qualify for extended weekends and vacations. You will start out with "diddly" and slowly build from there. So, you may have a little power plus a lot of responsibility and a great deal of work to do as well.

Not only are you responsible to the taxpayer, but your administration also deserves your best effort and loyalty. After all, they hired you... don't forget that. Not surprisingly, political loyalties can get very sticky and confusing. Your immediate boss may be your Secretary, Administrator or Chairman, but your ultimate boss is the President. At some point you may be faced with loyalty dilemmas and the choices you make will often depend on the potential conflict between your administration's political policies and your own personal views. That's a choice you will have to make at the time. Be assured, and please remember, that one of the reasons the administration hired you was for your support.

In addition to the loyalty issue you are obligated for everyone's sake, including your own, to remain within a very defined set of ethics and laws regarding your conduct. As a political appointee, you will sometimes be amazed at how non-political you are allowed to be. I won't get into an elaborate discussion of the rules at this point (see chapter 8), just be aware that many restrictions exist, and you will be schooled on them by your administration. Take this seriously. The rules are easy to follow, but the penalties for inappropriate behavior can be severe, both politically and legally.

As mentioned in the last chapter, the layers of

bureaucracy can be overwhelming. To get a decision on a relatively small matter can take forever. There is the relationship between the career employees and the appointees. Then there are the turf battles, power struggles and individual agendas found throughout the political chain of command. Yes, it's government. Turf battles can be found anywhere in life, but in government they are raised to an art form. While at HUD I became involved in a trivial turf battle. I was asked to coordinate the work between multiple departments on a specific project. One of my fellow appointees became irritated and claimed to our supervisor that he was more qualified than I to carry out this particular assignment. His selfish claim got him nowhere and it caused an unneccesary, long-lasting tension between the two of us. This was a shame. Again, you can deal with this as long as you know it is coming and you don't take it personally. I agree that this is often easier said than done but do your best. You can manage it.

Power struggles are similar to turf battles but with a subtle difference. The turf war is usually over issues and responsibilities. The power struggle will directly relate to position, job title, hierarchy and proximity to the top. This struggle can often be ruthless. To the uninitiated, this seems to be a strange phenomenon. Why would people of the same party, who have fought and worked hard to get their president elected, be at odds? Once inside, power can be obsessive and addictive. I gave serious thought to creating a chapter entitled "Egos;" I decided against it, but you get the idea. If you enter without warning, you will be disappointed. On the other hand, if you go in with your eyes open, you will be pleasantly surprised to find most of your fellow appointees will turn out to be very cooperative and likable.

Speaking of likable fellow appointees, once you

have your job, take advantage of as many of the social opportunities as possible. In addition to the international and national scenes, these opportunities could also include your state organizations, local social groups, sports leagues, etc. The people you meet while networking will be invaluable to your ongoing political experience. The strong, valuable relationships, as I continue to repeat, that will be formed are likely to continue for the rest of your life. This is a very special treat and will lead to many new opportunities.

Compensation is always a key factor with any job choice. Your starting salary will be a function of your job title. Each position will carry with it a salary range through the General Schedule pay scale for SC appointees. The SC scale contains approximately 15 grades and about 10 steps within each grade. This allows for an annual step increase, assuming a positive annual performance review. As an aside, the performance review, completed by your political superior, can often be more of a relationship review. Your raises and annual bonuses will likely depend on both. The higher pay grades within the SES and PAS have approximately five grades. Your entry level is somewhat negotiable within your given job title. So get advice from your supporters and just do your best. The actual pay relative to each grade varies every year. So stay in touch with these variances. See Chapter 3 for examples of actual dollar amounts of compensation.

Another key factor in your decision is lifestyle. Do you have a spouse and or children? Do you want to leave your home and move to Washington, D.C., which would most likely be more expensive than the place from which you are coming. Washington, D.C. is a beautiful city full of rich history, culture and entertainment, but it lives and breathes politics. Is this OK with you and your family? If your spouse is currently working, will it be difficult to find him/her a new job? What about a school change for your kids? Can you sell your present house without taking a financial hit? How long would you plan to stay? I know the answer to these questions is difficult, but you should address them and create at least a general game plan.

I'm happy to warn you that Washington, D.C. is full of people who intended to come for two years or so and then never leave. This is affectionately referred to as "Potomac Fever."

Why is this? It is quite simple. Washington, D.C. is the power center of the world. If you leave, what would you plan to do at the end of your appointment? Would you take your new knowledge and relationships and apply them back in your hometown or some other city? Or would you plan to stay in Washington, D.C. and apply them there? It's hard to predict the answers. But again, these questions should at least be given some thought. Keep in mind, though, that it is OK to have a plan going in and then alter it later if necessary. Lastly, you should think about why you are considering making the move to Washington, D.C. in the first place. Is it for patriotic reasons, political reasons, economic reasons, a career goal or some combination of these? What are your expectations? If you have some general answers to these questions, you can better decide whether or not the move and/or a particular appointment is for you.

COMPENSATION

So aside from the thrill and incredible experience, you think appointees should actually be paid. Well, you are correct. As touched on in Chapter 3, there are salary ranges for each category of political appointee. I will give you a general idea of the approximate amounts during various years but keep in mind they can change at any time, particularly after an election year.

As of President George W. Bush's administration presidents receive an annual salary of $400,000 along with a $50,000 non-taxable expense account. Compensation of the president is controlled by law within the United States Code, Title 3, Section 102.

In 2012, there were 321 PAS positions available. As mentioned earlier, the President has the authority to unilaterally appoint these people, with Senate approval, to high level positions within the federal government. In 2013, according to the Government Accountability Office (GAO), most of these PAS positions came with annual salaries of between $99,000 and $188,000 per year which included full federal employee benefits.

Presidential appointees not needing Senate approval (PA) are mostly appointed to commissions, councils, committees, boards or foundations. The PA's in the Executive Office of the President (EOP) directly support the President by providing advisory and administration services in areas such as foreign relations, U.S. and international economic policy and homeland security. According to the GAO, 99% of PA's are not paid a salary at all or are paid a daily rate of $635, or less, while actually serving.

Persons serving in SC positions are usually appointed by PAS and PA appointees rather than by the President. However, all appointments to Schedule C posts must be reviewed and approved by the EOP. As of 2013, Schedule C positions paid between $67,000 and $155,000 per year.

As mentioned earlier, Senior Executive Service (SES) positions are for the most part filled by career employees whose jobs are not likely to become subject to political appointment. The SES jobs are paid on a government set scale based on level and tenure.

DO YOU QUALIFY?

Realistically, the most important qualifications you can have are political experience and relationships within your particular political party. No matter what else you may have done in your life, how successful you may have been, how smart you are or how charming you may be, if you haven't been involved politically, you had better get involved RIGHT now.

There are two ways to do this: through your time or through your money. You have to give one or the other. If you can give both, so much the better. Get to know your county and state party chairmen and the active players within your political party. Work on campaigns for your local mayor, county commissioners, state representatives, senators and for your governor. Get involved in races for your congressmen and U.S. senators. And, for sure, volunteer for a presidential nominee. It is of particular significance if you commit to a candidate early on in the election process, i.e., during the primaries, assuming there is one. If your candidate wins the nomination, and then the general election, you have greatly enhanced your cause. But, it is still OK even if you end up on the wrong side of a given primary as long as you then pitch in and help in the general election. You are now a veteran and a known commodity.

The subject of political credentials reminds me of a friend of mine I will call Joe. Joe was working for a New York state senator and was applying for a Schedule C appointment at one of the federal agencies. He completed all the forms and did all the right things, including gaining the support of the agency's Deputy Secretary. His problem arose at the White House. Joe was on the White House computer database, which should be a good thing. But the White House Office of Personnel Management informed him that his "political stroke" was still pretty weak and he should prepare for a long wait. In this case, working for this particular state Senator, even from a large state, did not supply enough "juice" to get Joe an immediate position. He was patient, gained additional and stronger political support and eventually received his appointment. Joe did a great job and later moved to a successful staff career on the Hill serving as chief of staff for a U.S. Congressman. Joe's story is meant to illustrate the importance of political credentials and the competitiveness involved in the appointment process. His story also confirms the value of patience and persistence.

"Give your money" is self-explanatory. But what does it mean to "give your time"? Let's use a presidential campaign as an example. If you know someone working in the campaign at the national or state level, contact him/her and let him/her know about your interest in helping. Don't mention your interest in a future job as it would sound too self-serving. If you don't know anyone working on the campaign, I'll bet you have a friend who does know someone who is involved. Call the friend and ask for an introduction.

With up to three phone calls, you should hopefully be able to reach anyone. It's not only OK, but essential to learn to feel comfortable asking a friend for a favor. You would do the same for him/her and this is how connections are made and trust is built.

Once in touch with someone in the campaign, explain your background and your interest in joining the team. Send a resume and ask for an appointment to visit in person. This meeting may take place in your hometown or your home state at the candidate's office. Keep in mind, except for a very few senior campaign positions, your help will most likely be on a voluntary, unpaid basis. Remember this when discussing your time availability. When you have your personal interview, be enthusiastic and as informed as possible about the candidate, his/her opponent, the pertinent issues and the campaign in general. If you are hired, discover, with guidance from your supervisor, where you can be most effective and then get to work. Depending on your qualifications, your job may range anywhere from stuffing envelopes and manning phone banks to assisting with policy, fund raising, developing coalitions or possibly public speaking. Know your strengths and strive to show them off over the course of your volunteer work.

Regardless of your qualifications, do not give the impression that you are over-qualified for any of these activities. This is simply part of paying your dues. Meet as many people as you can and work hard. The people who get noticed in political campaigns are usually the ones who work the hardest. Well organized, professional campaign organizations will welcome and appreciate your initiative.

Back to giving money and a point of clarity: the money can be yours, which is wonderful, but many folks may not have that luxury. As a sign of good faith, do try to donate something, even if it is a minimal amount. But the raising of money from others for the benefit of the candidate is of tremendous value and very welcome. Because of the high cost of personnel and advertising, today's campaigns are more and more dependent on the big bucks and assisting in the fundraising effort is imperative. Speak with a candidate's campaign finance chairman for specific ways you can help. Raising money for your county, state and/or national party will also gain you positive recognition. Take some time to learn about effective fund-raising tactics, you will be happy you did.

If you happen to have experience in a particular area that is applicable to a specific job within an administration, this is certainly to your advantage. Professional qualifications are very important, but without political credentials as well, you will most likely be left at home. Let me repeat, it is critical to have a political supporter and/or mentor. If you have worked for a candidate or your political party in the past and have friends within the system, it would be quite advantageous to ask them to help promote your cause. Having multiple backers can only enhance your chance of success.

NOW WHAT?

If you have decided to go for it... congratulations! Now you need to get to work. Chapter 5 will purposely be somewhat repetitive, but that's because its message is so very critical for success. Your new dream can take awhile. It is government. It is politics. Contact your political friends, send them your resume and then wait for the phone to ring, and hope to set up an interview. If you haven't heard back within a week, it would be OK to contact your friends to get a status check. Again, begin by talking to as many people in the political world as possible.

In addition to national connections, this would include elected members and staff of your city, county and/or state government, including the governor, state representatives, senators, cabinet members, lobbyists, state and county party leaders and activists, county commissioners, mayors and city council members. And most importantly, be in contact with as many any members and/or staff of the current administration as possible. This would OBVIOUSLY depend on the political party in power at the time. Get dependable advice and win as many supporters as you can. Hopefully, through these various contacts, conversations and meetings, a number of valuable supporters will surface who are enthusiastic about your efforts and who will be willing to help you, especially if you have been able to help them in some way.

It helps to have a specific job in mind. Refer to *The Plum Book*. It will give you specific job titles and accompanying pay grades. You can also determine if a particular job is open. From this information, you can narrow your search.

It is easy for me to say, "narrow your search." This may or may not be difficult for you depending on your degree of knowledge about how the "system" works. I won't attempt to describe the detailed purpose and functions of all the agencies and departments listed in chapter 1, but I do want to give you a general overview of some of the primary ones.

In most cases, each agency's name will be somewhat definitive of its purpose. For example, the Department of State oversees our relations with foreign governments, the Department of Defense deals with our military and national defense and the Department of Transportation is responsible for our domestic transportation issues such as our national highway system. The Department of Justice is the legal arm of the executive branch and the Department of Commerce concerns itself with our country's domestic and international business policies. The Department of Education works at the national level to coordinate our primary and secondary education policies with various state and local authorities and the Department of Agriculture defines appropriate domestic policies regarding crops, livestock, etc. The Department of Labor works closely with labor unions and is concerned with workers' rights and conditions. The Department of Housing and Urban Development, in conjunction with the Federal Housing Administration (FHA), oversees our public and subsidized housing stock. The FHA produces and oversees home mortgages for low-income residents. The Department of Energy is in charge of our policies regarding all sources of energy including fracking, hydrocarbons and nuclear programs.

The Department of Treasury, with the cooperation of a few other agencies, sets fiscal and economic policy. The Department of Health and Human Services sets policy on issues concerning the prevention and cure of domestic health situations and the Department of the Interior oversees our national parks and forests. These are very broad definitions of some of the better-known government agencies that may be of interest to you. Many sources, such as the internet, the library, and personal friends with government experience are available to give you more detail.

Specific jobs within these agencies will vary. However, in most cases, below the Secretary, there will be an Assistant Secretary and a Deputy Assistant Secretary, having finite responsibilities. Some of the larger agencies will also have Under Secretaries responsible for broad department categories. Each of these positions will have Special Assistants assigned to them for additional support.

Be aware, that often times an agency Secretary will leave his position before the end of the four-year presidential term. The successor will sometimes bring in his/her own senior management which can possibly, because of the ripple effect, create additional turnover among the other political appointees throughout the agency. This turnover could be detrimental to you, but it should also be viewed as a potential opportunity.

Again, help your party and candidates in any way you can, particularly with the presidential campaign. Raise money... that speaks very loudly. Do as many favors as possible for your political network. At the risk of being even more repetitive, which is my intent, please remember that any financial donations you can personally make toward the cause is certainly an added plus. As I have stressed, meet and get to know as many people as possible within your party all over the country. You need to put in a lot of work with no real assurance of a job in the future. But if you are diligent, reliable, professional, consistent, loyal, and a team player, the odds will be with you.

Once again, be particularly attentive to your sponsors and supporters. These people are your most likely road to an appointment. They are the most important of all. In addition to your hard work, their recommendations will be of paramount importance.

IF YOUR TEAM WINS

Be quick and aggressive but not overbearing. Be persistent but still try to remain patient. There is a fine line here but use your common sense and do your best. It's OK to ask for what you want. You don't need to be bashful, just diplomatic. Listen well and show that you can take advice. It might also be a good idea to have more than one position in mind, in case your first choice doesn't pan out.

Have these discussions with your primary supporters. Ask them to make calls and write letters on your behalf to the White House Office of Personnel, and to the leadership of your desired agency, including the White House Liaison Office. Work on secondary support through personal contacts, letters and phone conversations. Have all of your support system contact the decision maker for your desired position.

Your quest should be at full speed ahead after the election victory, even before the inauguration. Your emphasis should be with the key campaign people and the transition team since few of the appointees will yet be in place. Don't forget to ask for the help of friendly senators and congressmen, particularly those who might have seniority on committees relative to your desired agency. Most importantly, have a "guardian angel" that will hand carry your papers through the system...actually, the more 'angels" the better. If not, your request may just go into the hole from hell along with thousands of other hopefuls. Ideally one would be at the White House Office of Personnel and another at your desired agency. Be sure to keep a complete copy of your file just in case it was to get lost somewhere in the system during your quest.

If your team loses, well, "stuff" happens. I'm sorry but if this discourages you, politics is probably not for you. Just keep working for your cause and sooner or later your time will most likely come. Don't quit. Don't be too "I" oriented. Be a team player, it will pay off in the long term. Your party and your supporters will probably need your help more than ever.

Attaining *A Plum Job* is summarized in this chapter, through these key points:

* Have a specific job in mind.
* Be early.
* Be persistent.
* Work on the campaigns.
* Primary supporters.
* Secondary supporters.
* Guardian Angels.

INTERNSHIPS

One often thinks of an internship as a great experience for students during summer vacations from college or even for a semester. Sometimes internships are paid positions but usually not. A political internship can be with, for example, a member of the House or Senate (including at the state level), at the White House, with a particular agency, one of the many Washington D.C. based think tanks, an association, a lobby firm, etc. I mention internships here simply because I think it is a healthy, exciting way for young people to be exposed to the political arena. They learn about their government, they meet influential people, they make new friends from around the country, they mature, and they have a lot of fun. For you parents out there, if one of your kids shows an interest, try to help them out. For you young people, talk to your friends who have been interns and speak to their parents. Internships are a great way to get a taste of government and politics early on in life and to gain insight into whether or not politics and a future political appointment might be of interest. If it is, go for it. A former intern certainly has as an inside track through his/her acquired knowledge of the system and the relationships that were developed.

8

HURDLES...
OVER THEM, NOT AROUND THEM

First of all, your team needs to win. Again, work your tail off during the campaign. After the victory, there will be a bunch of folks seeking a limited number of political appointments, most of whom will all have good credentials and strong supporters. Needless to say, the process will be competitive.

Let me quickly define competitive. If a new president has been elected, beginning the day after the election, his/her transition team will begin receiving an average of 5,000 resumes per day. Before this rate will begin to decline, four months will have passed and approximately 600,000 will have been received. These applicants are seeking political appointments with the new administration. Relate this to the approximately 4,000 total political appointments that will be available. The good news for you is that many of these people will not know as much about the proper procedure as you do.

As you are promoting yourself for a given position, be cautious with your trust. Politics can be a very fickle, power based, self-centered, what-can-you-do-for-me-today business. Be cautious of your new acquaintances. Pay attention to the difference between true friends, of which there will be many, and opportunists. Your friends will go to the mat for you, as you should for them. True friendships equal survival. Nurture them and cherish them. You will most likely have them for a lifetime.

As discussed earlier, many of the more senior appointments may require Senate approval. This can either be a rubber stamp process or an experience from hell. A good example of such a hellish approval process is the caustic strife that usually occurs during the Senate approval of Supereme Court Justices. Outwardly, the debate is centered around qualifications. In reality, politics plays a huge role in the process. The good news is that most of you will not be attempting to attain positions that require Senate approval. But for those exceptions, facts related to your personal life, career background, political history and most importantly, your political supporters, will be carefully examined. The White House and appointed aids will help you prepare for your confirmation hearing.

The necessary paper work required for any level of appointment can be overpowering. You will need to complete a personal background form that will include a 10-year job and residency history along with personal references. This form needs to be filled out in detail and, depending on the level of appointment, will be used as the basis for your required security clearance. If you are not exactly proud of your "rap sheet", you might again want to consider an alternative career path.

Also required will be a financial disclosure form,

which must be updated annually. Take this very seriously as well, and don't fudge. Less than total veracity can lead to serious legal problems. These forms are listed as hurdles not to scare you but to let you know up front that they will require a great deal of time. Completed fully and truthfully, they should give you no cause for alarm. The security clearance actually takes place after you have been hired. It can take months to complete. Problems arise in very few cases, especially if you are aware of the process before you apply. It is OK to have had past financial problems and not everyone in your past has to speak highly of you. However, criminal activities will most likely eliminate you from being able to obtain an appointment.

YOU GOT THE JOB...
NOW WHAT?

Work hard to earn your keep, be loyal to your team, listen to those with more experience, learn everything you can about the "system" and develop a positive relationship with the career staff. Typically, the more informed folks become the most valuable. Don't be afraid to speak up when you have the answers and ideas. Build a network of friends and interact with colleagues throughout the political spectrum.

Have a good time and enjoy the experience, make it meaningful. Maintain your original hat size. Remember how you got where you are... through politics. You may or may not have been the most qualified person for the job. But, you have it, so love it.

Politics will often drive policy. Don't fight it. It is fair to say that many agency programs are designed with political ramifications in mind. But in our representative form of government, with the separation of powers and a system of checks and balances, that's not to be unexpected.

Be aware of the legal and ethical boundaries you have inherited. You'll learn what they are and then stay within them. Specifically, I am referring in part to things such as taking outside work and/or income, disclosing confidential information to those not intended to know, purchasing assets such as stocks or real estate for personal gain based on your "inside" information, attempting to exert political influence on members of the Civil Service staff, political campaigning on taxpayers' time and the misuse of government assets for personal benefit. Again, experts from within your administration and agency will discuss these various responsibilities with you at length.

As I have mentioned earlier, make an effort to develop friendships with your political associates. In most cases this will come naturally. Be true to yourself. Use common sense. When in doubt about something, seek advice.

CHANGING POSITIONS WITHIN THE SAME ADMINISTRATION

After serving in a given position, it is natural to observe other opportunities of interest that may entail added responsibilities and greater pay. This might not happen, which is fine. But if it does, it's OK. Musical chairs are very common. People are constantly trying to upgrade their position. Hey, it's politics.

You may be aware of someone who is about to vacate a job that is of interest to you or a "plum job" may currently be open and you feel it would be a perfect fit for you. Quietly discuss this position with your trusted supporters inside and outside of your agency as well as any appropriate "friends" on the Hill. Depending on your relationships, you may also wish to go to the White House Office of Personnel.

If your desired position is within your current agency, the ask can be a little easier. Supporters at your agency, including the White House Liaison Office, will be able to help clear the way. Depending on the seniority of your position, your new role may not require active White House involvement to make a change. Though in some cases, the request could originate directly from the White House.

If your dream job is at a different agency, your task will be a little more laborious and take more time. The process is basically the same as above except that you will most likely be dealing with fellow politicos who may be unfamiliar with you. They will likely have their own relationships and agendas and quite possibly their own candidates for the position. If possible, you should discover what their agendas are and then create your own bond with these folks. You don't want them working against you, you want them supporting you. Again, be patient and continue to work hard at your current job. Hopefully, you are close to your current boss. In a perfect world, your current boss may not want to lose you, but he/she should still want what is best for you. Just remember that you are not in a perfect world,. You are in the world of politics.

A good friend, Jan, had been an SC at one of the cabinet level agencies for two years. Through her friendship with a senior member of the White House Personnel Office, she became aware of an SES position at a non-cabinet level agency that fit her private sector background. With the support of her current boss, she began an attempt to capture this new job.

In this case, her support came from the White House, not the new agency. The Administrator of the new agency had his personal support through a particular influential Congressman and it so happened that Jan had a close relationship with that Congressman's chief of staff. Through this friendship, she was able to arrange a meeting with the Congressman. This meeting lead to his writing a letter of support for Jan as well as making a personal call to the Administrator on her behalf. Jan then determined that a Senator from her home state, whom she knew, was the chairman of the committee that oversees her proposed agency. After meeting with the Senator, he also actively supported Jan.

She had the White House, a Congressman close to the Administrator and a strategic Senator all on her side. It took six months and a great deal of patience, but she got the job and she loved it.

WHEN TO GET OUT

Typically, you can expect to maintain your appointment for as long as your administration remains in office. If possible, it is desirable to obtain your appointment early on, even during the transition from the prior administration. This is when the A-Team is formed and many of the closest bonds of trust are developed. You would then share the camaraderie of being in the trenches at the always critical beginning. But that's not to say it isn't worthwhile to join at a later date. It's a little like going to a new high school your junior year. It can be fine, but in some cases, you wouldn't feel quite as close to your classmates as if you had enrolled at the beginning of the first year. On the other hand, if you begin perhaps two years into the term, some of the original players may have moved on by the time you arrive. So don' worry about it. The important thing to remember is that if you do a good job, you will fit in and be valued regardless of when you arrived.

Now that you are there, when should you leave? For sure you don't want to be the one turning out the lights for a departing administration. This is when every resume on the political planet will be on the street. Whether you are looking for another politically oriented job or using your political experience to land a "plum job" in the private sector, be ahead of the herd. This means you need to begin your search with plenty of lead time. If your President is about to complete his/her first term and is going to run for re-election, this can be very dicey. This situation will present you with a real judgment call. Will he/she win? If so, how much turnover will take place, etc. There is simply no stock answer here, consult with friends and use your best judgement.

If you are confident (confident being a relative term in politics) that your President is going to be re-elected, and your experience has been a positive one, you may, if asked, consider staying on board. But of course, there will be no guarantee of success. Many cabinet members, agency heads and other appointees could change even in an administration's second term. If you are one of these senior individuals and would like to continue serving in the new administration, your chance of success would, of course, be driven almost entirely by your political relationship with the new crowd. For those coming from a less than senior position, an abbreviated version of the original process of obtaining one's appointment may have to be repeated. But, if one has a strong relationship with key folks in the new administration, an appointment to the same or a new position should move along much easier than your original appointment.

12

HOW TO BENEFIT FROM YOUR POLITICAL EXPERIENCE

Unless you choose to remain in government by competing for and winning a career job or by receiving appointments in future administrations, you will eventually leave government service and return to the private sector. This might include consulting or lobbying, or it may be totally devoid of politics. In the past, you may have worked in the business world, education, the military, the practice of law or a multitude of other careers. After your experience in government, you may choose to return to your past profession while staying in Washington, D.C. or you may decide to relocate elsewhere. Regardless of your choice, you have enhanced your knowledge in specific areas as well as learning the intricacies of how your government and its political system works.

Perhaps the most added value is the many close relationships you will have developed both within the political world and within the career civil service corps in the various agencies. Wherever your future takes you, you will go with a sense of pride and satisfaction. You are also a richer person for having served your country.

If you choose to capitalize on your government experience in the private sector, there are many companies, trade associations, law, accounting, lobby firms, etc. that will place a high value on your expertise and relationships. This may be a financially rewarding step that might also allow you to remain politically involved. In fact, now that you are on the outside, you can in many ways become more politically active than when you were a political appointee inside the government.

Depending on the level of your prior political position, you may have a certain period of time when you are not allowed to lobby any agency you had worked with in the past. Such restrictions do not diminish your value because this rule, for good reason, applies to everyone. This restricted period passes quickly, and in the meantime you will have developed additional institutional knowledge and relationships that will prove invaluable.

13 AGAIN...
IS THIS FOR YOU?

After reading this guide, speak with friends who have spent or are spending time as a political appointee. Discuss it with your family, political acquaintances and supporters. Consider your family situation, career goals, financial status and what's in your heart. And remember, if you try without immediate success, you are no worse off than before. At worst, you have made new friends and learned a great deal about both the government and the political process that will likely pay you dividends in the future. And who knows, you may still end up with a political appointment in the future. If you really want it, don't quit trying.

This guide is meant to have drawn for you a detailed, easy to read road map of how to obtain a political appointment. You have hopefully developed a sense of government service, especially within the political arena, and what qualifications are required. I have tried to give you a step by step road map for realizing your wish of a political appointment, including overcoming the inevitable hurdles.

After receiving an appointment, I have suggested how to best conduct yourself in order to maximize your experience. Lastly, I have laid out some options as to when it might be best to leave and also how to capitalize on your political/government experience back in the private sector.

I hope I have stimulated your interest and equipped you with the tools and confidence to take action. Serving your country as a political appointee is an honor, it is exciting, and it is a unique learning experience. Yes, it can be frustrating at times, but the plusses far exceed the minuses. So, do yourself a favor and explore the idea. Then go with your heart and have fun!

ABOUT THE AUTHOR

After graduating from the University of Kansas, Mr. Anderson began his investment banking and real estate equity financing career with Paine Webber Jackson & Curtis in Kansas City. He was later asked to move to Tulsa to open and manage a new office for Paine Webber. He enjoyed this successful venture, but it wasn't long before the world of politics came knocking on his door. Mr. Anderson moved to our nation's capital in 1990 when he obtained a political appointment at the Department of Housing and Urban Development (HUD) under President George H.W. Bush and Secretary Jack Kemp where the world of public service awaited. He was later appointed to the position of Deputy Administrator of the General Services Administration (GSA). At the end of President Bush's Administration, Mr. Anderson remained in Washington, D.C. and re-entered the private world of residential real estate equity finance. In 2001 he returned to Kansas City. Mr. Anderson retired in 2010 and remains politically active.

GLOSSARY OF ABBREVIATIONS

67

EOP: Executive Office of the President

GAO: Government Accountability Office

GSA: General Services Administration

GS: General Schedule

NGO: Non-Governmental Agency

PA: Political Appointment without Senate Confirmation

PAS: Political Appointment with Senate Confirmation

PPO: Policy and Public Outreach

SC: Schedule C Appointment

SES: Senior Executive Service